100 Ways tc

For Sales Professionals, Entrepreneurs, and
Small Business Owners

100 Ways to Sell

For Sales Professionals, Entrepreneurs, and
Small Business Owners

Wes Young

Pageville Press

100 Ways to Sell

For Sales Professionals, Entrepreneurs, and Small Business Owners

Send all inquiries to: wesyoungbusiness@gmail.com

Pageville Press

ISBN: 978-0-9801907-2-4

First Edition

Table of Contents

Warning! This Isn't a Complete List

Before you get started with learning more about 100 ways to sell, I need to give you a warning.

Even though this book includes 100 ways to sell, this is far from a complete list.

The smartest way to use this book is to put as many of the things listed in the book as you can into use to immediately boost your sales, and to use the list to help you think of other ways to sell.

The truth is that there are 1,000's of ways to sell. As you go through all of the great ways to sell included in this book, keep a note pad and pencil or pen with you and write down any new ideas that come to you.

In other words, use this book as a starting point; not as an end point.

I know you're going to be successful as long as you never give up. Good luck in your sales journey!

The Basics of Selling – It's Not What You Think

If you want to know the inside secrets of being a great sales professional I'm going to share them with you here.

But before I do, I need to warn you that these secrets aren't what you probably think.

And I also want to urge you not to dismiss them because they sound so simple.

If you commit to using these sales secrets and use as many of the ways to sell listed in this book as you can, you're going to be one of the most successful sales professionals in the world.

And if your goal is to simply build some side income or a side business with your new sales skills, all you have to do is follow the same steps.

Here's sales secret number one:

People buy from people that they trust and/or like.

Here's sales secret number two:

Selling is about building a relationship with people.

No matter what you're selling or who you're selling to, it always comes down to selling to a person.

All you have to do is build relationships with people whose life can benefit or improve from what you're offering so they like and/or trust you.

This doesn't mean that you have to build deep relationships with every person who buys from you, but you do need to focus on relationships.

You're not trying to sell anyone anything. You're building a trusting relationship and offering products and/or services that are going to improve their lives in some way.

Here are the basic steps you need to follow to be successful in selling, no matter what you're selling.

Step 1: Build a relationship with as many people as possible.

Step 2: Focus on how you can help each person you build a relationship with. Identify how your products and/or services help each person and improve their lives.

Step 3: Build each relationship on trust, because this is the reason why they're going to buy from you.

Step 4: Use as many of the 100 ways to sell listed in this book to build relationships.

If you follow this simple step-by-step guide you're going to have all of the selling success that you can imagine.

You Can Sell

I don't know how many people I've helped over the years that didn't think they could sell. But the number is large.

The fact is that you can sell. People who believe that they can't sell think selling is about being deceptive or manipulating other people.

You learned the secrets of selling in the last chapter. Now you know that selling has nothing to do with what most people believe.

If you can build relationships with people and offer solutions that make their lives better in some way, you can sell.

Never tell yourself that you can't sell again. Instead, tell yourself that you're great at building relationships. Because you are already good at building relationships and this is all you have to do to be the best sales professional you can be.

You can sell!

All you have to do is follow the steps you learned in the previous chapter and use as many of the 100 ways to sell listed in this book as you can.

The only thing that can stop you is if you quit.

The Selling and Mindset Link

Being a successful sales person isn't about talent. Selling is about persistence and belief.

You already read about a simple selling system that works and about why you can sell. But you also need to believe that you can sell, and this is about your mindset.

Your mind controls everything that you do, and when you learn how to use your mind the right way you can use its incredible power to help you sell.

When you believe that you can sell it helps you continue selling through the times when things are tough.

You're going to have times when you're not selling as much as you want and it's going to be easy to start doubting yourself.

You can't give up, no matter what. You can't doubt your abilities, because if you do you might quit.

The worst sales person in the world is going to sell their product, if it's a good product, if they talk to enough people.

I know that you're not the worst sales person in the world. I know this because I know you can read and I know that you're reading this book to improve.

What this tells you is that if you follow the advice about selling in this book, and use as many of the ways to sell listed in this book as you can, and you never give up, is you're going to sell.

When you understand the sales secrets I shared with you earlier and use them, selling becomes a simple numbers game.

The more people you communicate with the more you're going to sell.

Decide right now that you can sell. Dedicate yourself to becoming a successful sales professional and commit to never giving up no matter what.

Go out and start building relationships. Build trust with your prospective customers.

If you're not selling a quality product or service, find a better one to sell.

A big part of your confidence in selling is your belief in your product or service. If you don't believe in your product or service it's going to show up when you're selling.

But when you have everything in place, all you have to do is communicate with enough people. This is why you have to commit to never giving up.

I'm going to share a goal system that I've used every time I've accomplished something important in my life.

You can use this system to accomplish anything important. This includes becoming the best sales professional that you can be.

Here's the system:

- Decide What You Want
- Commit to Getting What You Want
- Develop a Plan Based on What Others Have Done to Achieve What You Want
- Set an Action Plan and Follow It
- Take Action Immediately
- Take Action on Your Plan Daily
- Review Your Results and Adjust Your Plan

- Never Give Up

Free 5 Part Master Sales Course

You've learned that one of the secrets to being the best sales professional you can be is building relationships.

I want to continue building a relationship with you. This relationship started when you received this book. I want to build the relationship some more by giving you more value to help you become a better sales professional.

I've put together a 5 part master sales course that I want to give you for free.

It's delivered by email over the course of 5 days, and it's designed to take what you learn in this book and build on it with even more things to improve your results.

To sign up for your free 5 part master sales course simply go to 100WaysToSell.com and put your email in the box for the course and hit enter.

You're going to immediately receive the first part of the sales course and receive the next four parts over the following four days.

What to Sell

The truth is that it doesn't matter what you sell. I assume that you already have something to sell, or at least have an idea of what you want to sell.

I do recommend that what you sell is something that you believe in and it helps people in some way. But beyond this, the selling system that you learned earlier and the list of 100 ways to sell is all you need.

It might be hard to believe, but selling really is as simple as following the step by step system I covered.

You're going to get better at building relationships as you practice, but you're still going to have success as you're learning as long as you keep trying.

Once you learn that you do have the ability to sell, you're never going to have to worry about finding a job or how to make money again.

If you can sell you can find something to sell that can provide a good living for you and your family.

If you don't have anything to sell, or are looking for something to sell that half the population uses every day, and has high commissions, and lets you build residual income, I run a company that has something for you to sell.

Just drop me an email requesting details at wesyoungbusiness@gmail.com and I'll send you complete information.

1 – Call Everyone You Know

This might sound simple, yet many people who are trying to get started selling don't start by calling everyone they know.

I've heard all kinds of excuses around this, with the most common one being they don't want to bother people.

If what you're selling doesn't help improve other people's lives then you shouldn't be selling it.

And if your product or service does help improve people's lives, you should share it with everyone you know.

Even if they don't have a use for your product, if the product is good, they probably know people who can benefit from your product.

Don't over think this. Just pick up your phone, start calling everyone you know, and let them know what you're doing and how what you're offering benefits people.

If they're not interested, thank them for their time, ask if they can think of anyone who could benefit from what you have, and move on to the next person.

2 – Email Everyone You Know

This is a lot like calling everyone you know, but you use email.

Put together an email that you can send to everyone that you know that explains what you're doing and how your product or service can benefit the people who use it.

Depending on what you're selling, you can include complete details about your product or service or you can offer to send more information if they ask.

When I send emails about products that I offer I always let them know that they can call me if they want to learn more.

This way the people who prefer to use email can reply to the email and the people who prefer to talk can give me a call.

3 – Send a Letter

Many people think that regular mail is a thing of the past, but sending a letter is still one of the most powerful ways to sell.

Think about how many emails you get that you don't read. Now think about how many pieces of regular mail that you get and don't open.

If your letter doesn't look like junk mail there's almost a 100% chance it gets opened.

If you know the person you're sending the letter to, use a template much like the one you use for sending emails.

If the person doesn't know you, make sure to grab their attention quickly with a headline or strong greeting and an opening line that shows them an immediate benefit.

Make sure you give them complete details about how to order or get more information. I like to include my phone number so they can call me directly if they want to find out right now.

4 – Your Contact List

People used to keep a rolodex that had all of their contacts in it. Now most people keep a list of their contacts in their phone. And some people keep a list of contacts in their email program.

The point is that you should look in every place where you can find your contacts. The odds are good that you've missed many contacts when you started contacting people by phone, email, or letter.

Use your contact lists as a starting point to help you think of other people you know or have had contact with in the past.

The more people you can contact the more you're going to sell. And if you've had contact with them before you have a better chance of them responding to your contact.

5 – Family

When you think of selling something to your family you need to think about two things.

The first thing is if you're not confidant that what you're selling is something that can help your family members, why are you selling it?

Find something to sell that you believe in and that can truly make people's lives better in some way.

When you have a great product or service you want your family to have access to it so they can benefit.

The second thing you need to think about is all of your extended family. People usually don't think about all of their nieces and nephews, great aunts and uncles, and other extended family when they think of family.

If you're going to be the best sales professional that you can be you need to remember everybody in your family, even if you haven't talked to them or seen them for years.

6 – Friends

The same thing goes for your friends as I covered about your family in the last section.

You should have such a great belief in how your product or service helps people that you want your friends to benefit from it.

If you want to give your friends and family a discount because of your personal relationship with them, go ahead and do it.

But don't deny them a chance to get the benefits that your product or service can offer them. Let them decide if what you have is going to help them or not. They deserve the opportunity to make a decision for themselves.

7 – Co Workers

This one can be a little tricky because the person you work for might not like it if you spend too much time trying to sell things to the people you work with.

But there are many ways that you can let the people you work with know that you have something that can help them.

You can work it into conversations that you're making some extra money on the side with a side business or by talking about how you're using a new product that you happen to have available for sale.

Use your imagination to use your relationships with your co workers to offer them what you have to improve their lives.

8 – People You Buy From

Think of all the things you buy in your life and all of the people you buy from. If you're like most people you buy from dozens of businesses and people every year.

These people and businesses can be a great source of people to offer your products and services to.

Start making a list of everyone you buy from and every business you spend money with.

Remember that businesses are owned by people and run by people. If you have a product or service that fits a business that's great. But you still sell it to a person for the business.

And even if your product or service is more personal, the people owning or running or working in each business are prospects.

9 – Clubs You Belong To

Social clubs aren't as popular as they used to be, with many social things moving online. But if you belong to and participate in any clubs, these can be great places to offer great products and services.

You might even have the opportunity to donate something you sell to the club or through the club to get some goodwill and cheap marketing for your business.

You don't have to be pushy to introduce your products to club members. Remember that you're in the relationship building business first, and the sales will follow.

10 – Door to Door

Door-to-door selling is a tough business, but it's also the absolute best place to learn what works and what doesn't work in selling.

If your product or service is something that can be sold door-to-door, pick a decent neighborhood and start knocking on doors.

Be prepared to be told no a lot, but learn something from every opportunity. And if you're persistent, you're going to find some buyers.

Door-to-door selling is a numbers game. You have to be willing to knock on a lot of doors, but if you have a good product and pick the right neighborhoods you can do well.

When you do sell to someone using door-to-door selling, make sure to ask for anyone they know who might benefit from your product or service.

Referrals are a great way to go from a cold call to a warm call situation.

11 – Flea Markets

Depending on your product or service, a flea market might be the perfect place to find people you can help with your product or service.

Most people only think about selling products at a flea market, but you can set up at a flea market and talk to people and get leads for higher priced products or services.

You need to be outgoing and strike up conversations with people as they pass by. Make sure you have a colorful banner or signage and plenty of brochures or other sales literature about what you offer.

A flea market is also a great place to offer a drawing for a free product. Have people sign up for the drawing at your stall and then you have a large list of prospective buyers to follow up with.

Communicate with all of the entrants who didn't win and offer them a discount.

12 – Craft Malls

Most people who sell things that aren't crafts don't think they can get in a craft mall. But I've sold plenty of things that aren't crafts in craft malls over the years.

The main difference between craft malls and flea markets is that you place your products or information in the craft mall and you aren't there when people shop.

Even if you don't sell products you can place a display for your service in a craft mall that can generate leads for your business.

The key is designing a display that catches the eye of people who pass by and quickly and clearly shows the benefits of what you're selling.

13 – Antique Malls

For the most part antique malls and craft malls are about the same. You need to use the same techniques when you put a booth in an antique mall as you use in a craft mall.

If you sell products, they don't have to be antiques, but it can help if you can tie your products to the people looking for antiques in some way.

But I've sold new products in antique malls that don't have anything to do with antiques.

At the end of the day, the more eyeballs you can get on your products or services the better your chance of finding the people you can help the most.

14 – Yard Sales

When you think of a yard sale the odds are that you think of someone else's junk. But you can sell new things at yard sales as well.

In fact, depending on what you're selling, you might be able to sell your products at full price.

Think about the types of people who go to yard sales all of the time. Does your product or service offer benefits to these people?

In my area, the majority of people who visit yard sales on a regular basis are female and tend to be a little older.

Of course, these aren't the only people who visit yard sales.

You can set up your own yard sale and you can ask people you know who are doing a yard sale if you can put a few of your products in their sale.

You can even offer them a small commission or a gift for their help.

15 – Yard Signs

Have you seen signs in yards and along the road offering employment, internet service, or real estate?

Why can't you put up some signs for your product or service?

When you use yard signs make sure that the writing is big enough so it's easily readable when people drive by.

You also need to show what you're offering in as few words as possible.

Put a phone number and a web site address on the sign so people have more than one way to contact you if they're interested in what you're offering.

16 – Church Members

Members of your church are usually a good source of people you already have a relationship with that you can offer something to.

I contact these people outside of church by phone, email, or direct mail so I keep my business out of the church, but you can do this based on your relationships with them.

If you give a portion of the profits from your selling business to the church or some other worthy cause, make sure that people know this when you're building a relationship.

17 – Bulletin Boards

Many businesses have bulletin boards in their entries and these are great places to pin up business cards, flyers, or brochures.

I like to go with a bright color so that it stands out.

You aren't going to have much space so you need to describe the benefits of your product or service in a few words. Pictures can help in this area a great deal.

Another tip is to bring your own tacks and tape with you when you head out to put things on bulletin boards.

Pay attention to every business you go in to see if they have a bulletin board. Sometimes libraries and other places that aren't considered businesses also have boards where you can put things up.

18 – Billboards

This depends a great deal on your product or service, but if it lends itself to billboard advertising you can get some good deals in some parts of the country.

Billboard advertising isn't as popular as it used to be and there are almost always open spots available.

If you see an empty billboard close to where you live, call and see what the owner is willing to offer.

If the billboard has been empty for long, make a counter offer when they give you a price. The owner isn't making any money at all when the space is empty, so they might take less than they ask to create some cash flow.

Remember that people who see billboards don't have much time as they drive by. Make your offer big and clear and give them an easy way to contact you.

19 – Have a Sales Party

Think of all of the products that have been sold over the years in a home party environment.

Everything from make up to baskets to Avon to Tupperware has been sold using parties.

Instead of instantly deciding that what you have to offer won't work in a home party, take a few minutes to brainstorm possibilities.

The main business that I own that people sell for is a line of beauty products. These products sell extremely well using home parties.

(If you're interested in learning more about this opportunity, send me an email.)

When you do home parties, come up with a way to offer prizes, even if they aren't directly related to your product.

It's also a good idea to provide snacks and drinks.

20 – Pass out Flyers

Flyers are an inexpensive way to get the word out about the products or services that you offer.

You can print flyers at home or get them done cheaply at a local office store.

Then your only cost is your time finding places to put them and hand them out. And when you pass flyers out make sure that you spend time building relationships with people you meet.

When I'm in full selling mode like when I'm launching a new product, I carry a stack of flyers with me everywhere I go.

You can also ask your family and friends if they can think of anywhere that you can put up or hand out flyers.

21 – Teach a Class

One of the best ways to sell products or services is to be recognized as an expert. People tend to trust people that they think are experts, so anything you can do to appear to be an expert is valuable.

Is there anything that you can teach that has anything to do with your product or service?

I spend some time doing business consulting and have taught business classes at a local college that proved to be a good way to acquire new clients.

If you sell anything beauty related you could teach a course on matching products to your skin type.

If you sell insurance or real estate, you could do a class about nontraditional ways to invest.

Do some brainstorming to see if you can come up with a subject that people are interested in that relates to what you have available for sale.

22 – Tag Line in Emails

This is a simple thing that everyone who sells anything should do. It only takes a couple minutes to set up and you let people know you have a great product or service available.

Simply go into your email settings and set your signature or tag line. Once you set it up, it automatically attaches to the end of your email every time you send one.

If you post in forums or elsewhere online you might be able to do the same thing.

23 – Decal on Your Vehicle

You can buy a decal to put on your car that advertises your products or service. Many places will make a magnetic sign for your car door or for the back of your truck or SUV.

This is a great way to advertise whenever you drive anywhere. And once you get it made and installed on your vehicle you don't have to think about it again until someone sees it and contacts you about what you're offering.

Just like some of the other things in this book, you need to use big letters and a simple message.

People won't be able to look at your sign for long as you drive by, so make it easy to see what you offer and how to contact you.

24 – Place Mat Ads

Many mom and pop type restaurants use place mats, and some of these place mats have ads for other businesses on them.

People have time when they eat and most of them will at least take a look at the place mat if it has something interesting on it. This makes it a great place to let people know what you have available.

Ask someone at the restaurant who to talk to about placing an ad.

You aren't going to have a great deal of space for your marketing message, so keep things short and simple.

Give the readers a quick snapshot of what you offer and the best benefits and then a way to order or contact you. This is all you need to catch the eye of prospective buyers.

You can also include a coupon in your ad to boost response.

25 – Business Cards

Business cards are a good way to introduce yourself and your business to people, but don't think of business cards the same way as everyone else uses them.

A business card has a lot of space on it that most people don't use, and there's a back that you can print things on as well.

Use both sides and all of the space on both sides to your advantage.

This does two important things. The first thing is it lets you share more information and do more to build a relationship.

The second thing it does is make you and your business card stand out from every other business card, because you're doing something different.

26 – Brochures

People don't use brochures as much as they used to, but they're still a great way to start and build your relationship with prospective buyers.

Make sure that your brochure is filled with information that's useful to your prospective customer.

Fill it with benefits and how using your product is going to improve your prospect's life.

You can also use some of the space in your brochure to explain how to use your product or service if applicable.

Don't make the mistake of talking too much about you in the brochure. Spend most of the space talking about them, because this is what they care about.

27 – Do a Press Release

Press releases aren't as popular as they used to be, but they've always been a way to get free media coverage.

And any type of media coverage is going to help you sell more of your products and services.

The key is to frame your story in a way that's appealing to the news media. This might take some brainstorming, but it's worth the effort.

A successful press release can also lead to radio and television interviews, which help you sell more.

Nationwide press releases can be good, but if you're selling on a local level contact all of your local media.

You can send out a press release yourself or you can use a service that distributes it for you. I've used services in the past because it's a lot of work to send your own out unless you're just targeting local media outlets.

28 – Ads on Buses

If you live close to a city that uses a bus system, contact the city to find out who owns and runs the busses.

Placing an ad on the side of a bus is a great way to get a wide range of exposure for your business.

Make sure that you create a short powerful message because people might not get to see it for long as they drive past.

You also want to make your message as big as possible, and don't forget to give a simple way to contact you about your product or service.

29 – Yellow Pages

Most people forget that every business used to be listed in the yellow pages. They don't think anyone uses the yellow pages anymore because of the internet, but you're missing out on an important market for your business.

If your products and services are of interest to older people you need to find out if you still have a local print phone book and see if you can get an ad in the yellow pages.

Many people in the older generation are hesitant to use the internet for a lot of things and they've been using the yellow pages their entire life.

Don't miss out on the opportunity to sell to this important group of people.

30 – Offer Coupons

Coupons are a great way to introduce your product or service to new customers.

Everyone wants to get a deal, and a coupon might be just the thing that moves someone who's considering your business into becoming a customer.

Make your coupon simple and easy to understand and distribute it everywhere you can think of.

Put a coupon on your flyers, brochures, and on the back of your business card. If you have a web site for your business, put a coupon on the main page.

You can also give extra coupons to friends and family members and ask them to give them to people they know. This is an inexpensive way to get free exposure and create new customers.

31 – Put It on a Calendar

Have you ever picked up a free calendar at a bank or other business that you visit?

If you have, the odds are that you've hung the calendar somewhere and looked at for the next 12 months.

You can have calendars printed with your business as the main attraction and stay in the front of your potential customer's mind for the next year.

The next time your potential customer needs or wants what you have to offer the odds are good that they're going to think of you first because they see your business every time they look at the calendar.

32 – Put It on a T-Shirt

It used to be expensive to get custom t-shirts made because you had to pay a set up cost and place a minimum order.

Now you can buy one shirt at a time or place a small order and not invest a fortune.

You can have t-shirts printed that you wear, give them to your friends and family, give them away when you're doing other marketing, or run a contest and use them for the prizes.

When people wear your t-shirt they're giving you free advertising.

Another secret you can use if you have enough margins with your product is to give a free t-shirt with each order.

This gives you free advertising and your customer is getting something free with their order.

33 – Put It on a Coffee Mug

This is basically the same idea as putting your business on t-shirts. But many people drink coffee every day, so if you put your business on a coffee mug they're going to see your business every day.

Instead of simply putting your business name on a coffee mug, put a coupon or an offer on the mug.

This will make your mug stand out from other mugs and give people a reason to contact you.

Give as many coffee mugs away as you can to people who are in your target market. This is another great way to stay in the front of the mind of your potential customers.

34 – Classified Ads

Classified ads are one of the most inexpensive ways to get the word out about your product or service.

You can run classified ads in your local papers or contract to have them placed in papers in certain states or nationwide.

You can also run classified ads in some magazines. Check out the back of magazines that your target market reads to see if they have a classified section.

When you start using classified ads, make sure you have an opening that grabs reader's attention.

Make your message as powerful as you can in just a few words. You can sell some products directly in classifieds, but some products require more information.

Give readers an easy way to contact you to receive more information.

35 – Space Ads

Space ads can be placed in newspapers and in magazines, as well as on many web sites.

The key is making a great ad that grabs your prospect's attention and placing your space ads in publications that your target market reads.

Unlike classified ads, you can include pictures and graphics in space ads.

Space ads are usually more expensive to run than classified ads, but you can get more space with a space ad and they're usually in a better spot in the publication than the classified ads.

Your ad can get lost in the classified ads because there are so many other ads, so it's easier to grab attention with a space ad.

36 – Newspaper Ads

Newspaper ads come in all shapes and sizes. You just learned about classified ads and space ads, but there are other types of newspaper advertising available as well.

Contact your local newspaper and ask them about their available ad packages. Many newspapers offer inserts, which is a great way to get a bigger ad that stands out from the ads that are placed on the pages of the newspaper.

I also recommend putting together a press release about your business, like I covered in another chapter, and ask the newspaper to run it for free when you place an ad.

This is a great way to get extra exposure when you start placing ads in newspapers.

37 – Newspaper and Magazine Articles

If you're a decent writer you can start writing articles for newspapers and magazines that have something to do with your product or service.

You have to learn how to write in the style they want and you can't overly advertise your product or service in the articles, but you can learn how to do this in a way that provides good information to the reader and points to you or your product or service as a possible solution.

Writing articles for newspapers and magazines also helps position you as an expert, and remember that people buy things from people they trust.

If your prospective customers view you as an expert it makes it easier for them to buy from you.

38 – Magazine Ads

Magazines are a better place to run your ads than newspapers for many products. But magazine ads usually cost more than newspaper ads.

However, ads in magazines tend to get a better response than ones placed in newspapers. Even though most magazines have a lot of ads, they still usually have fewer ads than newspapers.

This makes it easier for your business ad to stand out and grab people's attention.

I'm a strong believer in getting as much information in an ad as you can, but you also need to make sure that your ad is clear and easy to read.

Make a list of magazines that your target customers read and contact them to get advertising options and rates.

39 – Radio Ads

It depends on the type of product that you offer, but radio ads are a great way to find new customers for many types of products and services.

People who listen to the radio are a captive audience, but you still need to do something with your ad that grabs their attention right away.

Focus on explaining how your product or service makes their lives better and give them a reason to contact you immediately.

I like to run a special deal for radio listeners that expires soon. Give them a promo code to use when they order or contact you.

You can hire a local radio personality to voice over your ad or you can do it yourself. I like to do my radio ads myself because it helps make the listener think they know me better.

40 – TV Ads

TV ads used to be extremely expensive to run, but now there are 1,000s of channels and you can find good deals on these ads.

If you're focusing on your local market, contact all of your local television stations and cable companies and ask what kind of advertising packages they offer.

You might even be able to do your own informational television show on small local networks.

I did a weekly show on a local TV station and was able to reach a lot of people that I'd never have reached any other way.

Just like radio ads, I prefer to appear in my own TV commercials because it builds trust and a relationship. But you can hire someone to do your commercial or put together a slide show and you do the voice over if you don't want to appear on camera.

41 – Do a Seminar

A good way to position yourself as an expert is to do a seminar.

Come up with a subject that's related to your product or service that you know a lot about and start advertising your seminar.

You can also contact your local library, chamber of commerce, and colleges to see if they might be interested in hosting your seminar.

The best thing about seminars is you don't even have to sell too hard during the seminar. If you give your attendees good information, some of them are going to want to talk to you about solutions.

Give a good seminar and simply announce that you have a solution available and will stick around to talk to anyone who is interested.

42 – Do a Workshop

A workshop can be a lot like a seminar, but when you use the word workshop instead of seminar it might be received better by some people.

The main difference between a seminar and a workshop in many people's eyes is a workshop is more hands on.

This is easy to do, even if you design a seminar. Simply build some practical exercises into your program and possibly put together a workbook that attendees can use during and after the workshop.

You don't have to do a workshop exactly about your product or service. Create a workshop that solves a problem that people have or that makes their lives better that can use your product or service as the solution or part of the solution.

43 – Write a Book

Nothing positions you as an expert like writing a book. Authors are considered experts by many people, even if they aren't the top expert in the world.

You know that people buy from people they like and/or trust, and being considered an expert is about as good as it gets from a trust standpoint.

The book you write doesn't have to be exactly about what you're selling. It just has to have something to do with it.

If you're selling high ticket items, you can use your book instead of a business card. Imagine how much more power you have when you hand a prospect your book instead of a business card.

I recently used this exact strategy to close a $4,000 deal.

This is one way to separate yourself from any and all competition.

44 – Write an EBook

At one time ebooks didn't carry the same weight as normal books, but they're much more common now.

You might not gain quite the authority status writing an ebook as writing a regular book, but you're still going to be viewed as an authority by many people.

The upside of writing an ebook is once you complete the book you can distribute it for free.

Write an ebook dealing with your product or service and how you offer a solution that improves your customer's life.

Then give free copies of your ebook to as many people as you can think of. Ask all of your friends, family, and contacts to give your ebook away or let you know who they know that can benefit from reading it.

45 – Create a Special Report

People are always interested in information if you present it in the right way. People have pain in some area or areas of their life and they're looking for solutions.

People are also looking for things that make their lives better in one way or another.

Remember these things when you come up with a title for your special report. Use a title that either tells people you can help them with some form of pain, or that tells them their life is going to be better after reading your information.

Once you complete your special report, send it to everyone you know and ask them to forward it to anyone who can benefit from it. Or you can sell it for a low cost and use it to generate paid leads.

When you help people with their pain and problems, or make their lives better, they're more likely to buy from you.

46 – Write a White Paper

White papers are a lot like special reports, but they usually are aimed at businesses or industries instead of individual people.

But remember that businesses are owned and run by people, so you're still writing to a person.

You just need to cover a topic that relates to business or industry in some way when you write a white paper.

With a little bit of imagination and brainstorming you can do both a special report and white paper using the same subject matter.

Once you finish your white paper, contact as many businesses as you can that it relates to in any way and offer to send them a free copy.

47 – Consignment

This is a great way to get products in front of new people. Here's how it works:

You approach local business owners and offer to provide your product for no cost up front. When they sell your products they pay for them.

It depends on how much margin you have, but you have to offer a decent incentive for the store owner to display your products. I recommend at least a 20% discount, and a higher discount will get more owners to agree to display your products.

This is a low cost way to get new customers. While some customers will go back to the store where they bought your product when they want to buy again, if you have a way to order direct on your product, some of them will buy direct.

Make a list of all of the locally owned businesses in your area where your product fits and start asking.

48 – Sell Direct to Businesses

You can also sell your products direct to businesses instead of offering them on consignment.

Start with local businesses and expand out from there. All you need to do to get started is to approach local businesses and offer your products.

You need to decide if you're willing to offer payment terms before you start selling direct to businesses.

If you give them 30 or 60 days to pay you have a better chance to find businesses that are willing to buy from you. But there's also some danger in doing this, because when a business starts to struggle they might be slow to pay, and if they go out of business you might have a hard time getting your products back.

49 – Sell in Bulk

Selling in bulk is a lot like selling direct to businesses, but it also can include placing your products with distributors and wholesalers.

This can be tricky to get started and you need to make sure you have enough inventory to supply what these types of businesses need.

You also are probably going to have to front the product and wait to get paid, so if you don't have enough cash reserves this can put your business at risk.

But the upside is that distributors and wholesalers can open your business up to new places to carry your products.

Look for local wholesalers and distributors first and go talk to them to learn more. Once you learn from them you can approach larger companies that have a broader reach.

50 – Sponsor an Event

This is one of my favorite ways to get free or low cost marketing and publicity.

Events run in communities all around the world all of the time. And sometimes you can get involved by simply donating a few of your products for prizes.

You can also sponsor an event with a monetary amount. If you do this make sure you know what type of exposure you're going to get.

Look for events where people you want to get exposure to are likely to be.

A few places to look that hold events are schools, churches, cities, counties, and local businesses.

51 – Do Something Newsworthy

Getting in the local newspaper and on the local TV news can give you a fast boost in sales. But you have to do something that's newsworthy and make sure the local news media knows about it.

Use your imagination to see what you can come up with that the news media might be interested in.

For example, if you're sponsoring a local event make sure to let the news media know about it. Or donate some products or money to a local business that helps people like a food bank or shelter and let the media know when you're going to do it so they can send someone out to cover it.

You can also donate your time to important local causes that can get you some free news coverage.

Brainstorm some ways that you can help other people and get free news coverage at the same time.

52 – Point of Purchase Displays

When you go in a business and go to the check out area, often you see products available either on the counter or close to the counter.

Think about going through the checkout line when you buy groceries. These are called point of purchase displays.

Depending on your product, you might be able to buy a display of some sort that you can display your products in.

Then all you have to do is ask store owners if you can place your display in their store.

I've found that combining this with a consignment agreement, which you read about in an earlier chapter, makes it easier, but you can also do this selling the display directly to the business.

53 – Repeat Sales

The most profitable sales you make are going to be to your previous customers, as long as you take good care of them.

This all starts with making sure that they know exactly how to buy from you again. You need to have ordering information on or included with everything that you sell if it's at all possible.

You can also offer free information to buyers about how to use your product and/or keep them up to date on specials and promotions.

Offer coupons to customers that sign up for your list, whether it's a direct mail list or using email.

You need to focus on making sure that every customer is happy and feels that you care about them. This will make them come back and it will make them tell other people about you and your business.

Do everything you can to encourage repeat customers.

Start with a quality product or service, give the best service after the sale that you can, and follow up with your customers frequently.

54 – Run a Contest

People love to enter contests that give them an opportunity to win something for free.

You can take advantage of this by creating contest and using your product as a prize.

Not only does this help you get more attention for your product, but it also gives you a list of people to market to in the future.

If your product or service isn't exactly right for a contest, come up with something related that you can run a contest for.

You don't have to design every contest as a simple entry and drawing. You can run a contest where entrants do something or submit something.

55 – Package with Other Products

This is a powerful way to sell your products if they're similar to other products or if you're facing a lot of competition.

You can package your products together to make a unique package that can't be found anywhere else, or you can package your product with someone else's product or service.

The key is to differentiate your product from everything else on the market. If you're selling basically the same thing as others are selling, you can create unique options that no one else is offering.

You can also approach other successful people selling something that your product complements and set up a package that includes your product and theirs.

This is going to introduce you to new customers by associating your product with an already successful product or brand.

56 – Consulting

Does your product relate in any way to something that people or businesses need or use?

When people hear the word consulting they often think of business consulting. But this is like living with blinders on.

Many different types of consultants operate and help people and businesses every day. I've seen beauty consultants, dating consultants, and life skills consultants.

If you can start offering consulting services that are in some way related to your product or products you're going to sell more.

Not only will you sell your products to the people you offer consulting to, but this is another way that you position yourself as an expert.

Another trick that you can use is package consulting with your product or service.

57 – Coaching

It seems like everywhere you look, someone is offering their coaching services. You can find a coach for just about anything in your life.

Coaching is a lot like consulting, but it's often an easier sale to people that don't run a business. People seem to think that businesses need consultants and people need coaches.

Just like consulting, figure out a way to offer a coaching service that has something to do with your product or service.

If you can't come up with a better idea, consider offering life coaching services. Everyone is living life and looking for ways to get better results, feel better, and be more successful.

Also just like consulting, if you're offering coaching services you're positioning yourself as an expert, which helps more people trust you and buy from you.

58 – Free Reports

You've read about different types of things you can write to position yourself as an expert in other chapters.

Some of those things, like books, ebooks, and white papers can be sold or given away.

A free report is simply a short written sales tool that isn't a sales letter. You put together 1 to 5 pages or so that gives people valuable information and introduces your product or service as a solution.

It's easy to give away free reports by email, and you should do this, but I've found it more powerful to print them out and hand them to prospective customers or mail the free report to them.

You can even offer free reports with the sale of your products as a way to build perceived value for your products.

59 – Run a Sale

Everyone likes to get a deal. People are much more likely to buy your product when they think they're getting a deal. So give them an extra reason to buy.

You should be able to show people that your product offers more value than it costs, which is the only way that anything gets sold.

But you can show them even more value by running a sale.

And a sale doesn't even have to be big. Sometimes 10% off is enough to get someone who has been thinking about trying your product or service to make the decision to finally buy.

This is an extremely powerful sales tool if you have a product that people consume and need more of on a regular basis.

You get them to try the product for a reduced price and they like your product and become consistent buyers.

60 – Free Shipping

The biggest draw that Amazon has with their Prime membership is free shipping. They have millions of items that ship for free to Prime members and they have millions of Prime members.

You can use this same sales technique by simply offering free shipping for your product, no matter where you sell it.

Even if you have to adjust your pricing so that you can offer free shipping it's usually a good idea.

Many people would rather pay $25 for a product with free shipping than pay $15 plus $10 shipping for the same product.

If you can't afford to offer free shipping on every order, set an order limit that unlocks free shipping.

For example, if you sell $10 products, offer free shipping on all orders over $50 or $100.

61 – Gift with Purchase

Many sales systems have been built and grown over the years using a free gift with purchase. And the amazing thing is the free gift doesn't even have to have anything to do with the product that the person buys.

Of course, it's always better if your free gift has something to do with your product, but if you can't come up with anything related find something else.

One of the simplest and least expensive options is to give free reports about how to use your product with every purchase.

You can also offer a free video explaining and showing how to use your product or a CD or an audio file delivered by email.

Use your imagination to come up with something that adds perceived value to your customer that you can give as a gift with each purchase.

62 – Movie Theater Ads

The last time you went to see a movie I bet you saw some ads on the screen before the movie started.

Is your product or service of interest to people who go to the movie theater?

You're going to have some up front production costs to shoot your commercial just like if you run TV ads, but this is a one time cost. And if you're already running TV ads you can often use the same commercial.

Ask the manager at the movie theater for more information about placing an ad for your product or service on screens before movies.

63 – Newspaper Inserts

You learned about different types of newspaper advertising in other chapters like classified ads and space ads, but one of the most effective ways to use newspapers for advertising is inserts.

Newspaper inserts are the loose leaf pages that are usually inserted when the newspaper is folded.

Most of them are a single page, but you can do a bigger insert if your product or service requires more space.

People are much more likely to see an insert than a space ad or classified ad, but they know that inserts are ads so you need to design your insert in a way that quickly catches their attention.

Use a big bold headline and focus on the big benefit or benefits of your product or service and include a coupon and easy way to order or contact you for more details.

64 – Direct Mail Inserts

Direct mail inserts are similar to newspaper inserts except they're delivered by mail. You likely used to receive packages of coupons and advertisements on a regular basis this way from companies like Valpak.

Many areas still receive direct mail inserts once a week folded into a larger ad or an advertising newspaper type thing.

You can also contract with companies that are already selling products to your market to have them ship your inserts with their products.

A few magazines also offer inserts for advertisers, so make sure to ask if you're running ads in magazines or writing articles for magazines.

65 – How to Videos

It used to cost a lot of money and take a lot of time to produce a video. But with the technology available today you can shoot a high quality video without spending much money and in a short time.

Many phones have the capability to shoot high quality videos and you can use free software available online to edit them.

You can use how to videos as sales tools by posting them online or sending them directly to customers and potential customers.

Or you can produce a how to video and include it or a link to it for free when someone buys your product.

You can also do informational how to videos about something related to your product and offer your product as a solution to the prospective customer's needs or problems.

66 – How to Report

One of my favorite things to give for free when someone purchases a product is a simple how to report.

How to reports are short written reports that explain how to use your product. You can print them and include them with your product or you can post them online and include a link to them with your product.

And just like how to videos, you can do a how to report about something related to your product and offer your product as a solution.

People search for information about how to do things all of the time. Take advantage of this by producing how to reports about as many things related to your product as you can.

Make your how to reports available in as many places as possible and use your friends and family to help you get them out to people who need them.

You can even sell how to reports for a low cost to generate leads for your products and services.

67 – Information Products

Information products are any type of product that's built on information. They can be written, digital, video, audio, or a combination of two or more of these things.

You can use information products to help market and sell your products and services or you can build an entire business around selling information products.

People pay for information in order to save time, improve their lives, or make their lives easier.

Build information products that offer valuable information around your products and/or as a way to make your products more valuable.

You might be able to add a new revenue stream to your current business by launching an information product line.

If you're interested in developing an information product business, see the chapter at the end of this book for entrepreneurs.

68 – Solve a Problem

In a perfect world your product or service solves a problem or problems. People want solutions to problems in their life.

If your product or service doesn't solve a problem, try to figure out a way you can position it so that it is a solution for a problem.

Look for problems that you have or that your friends and family have and see if you can position your product or service as a solution.

If you're looking for new products or services to sell, look for problems that already exist. Figure out a way to solve these problems and you have a great product or service to sell.

69 – Create a Problem

Sometimes people have problems that they're not doing anything about or that they don't even know that they have.

This can be a powerful marketing tactic if you can use your marketing and advertising to show people that they have a problem.

Once you educate them about the problem, you offer your product or service as the solution to the problem.

If you can show people how your product can help their pain, whether this is physical pain or mental pain, you can sell more.

This might take some brainstorming, but try to identify problems that your product solves that people are either ignoring or don't know that they have.

Then start educating them and offering what you have to solve these problems.

70 – Add on Sales

One of the best ways to boost your profits and sales is to sell more when you sell a product or service.

If you have more than one product that you sell, make sure that you offer additional products every time someone buys a product.

If you don't have any products to add on at the time of sale you should either add products to your inventory or develop products that you can use as add on sale.

Information products are a great option for add on sales because they have a low cost and can be positioned in a way that they show a large value.

You should do everything you can to sell more to the people that you're already selling to because they already trust you enough to do business with you.

71 – Money Back Guarantee

People are afraid of making a mistake, and they often don't buy something because they're afraid it's the wrong decision.

Offer a money back guarantee on your products to help your potential customers feel safe.

If you can make them believe that there's no risk, they're more likely to make the decision to buy.

If you're providing a high quality product you're not going to have to deal with many returns. And when you do get a return you have the opportunity to build goodwill and create a long time customer.

A tactic that I've used with success is when someone contacts me about returning a product I immediately process the refund and ask them to please give the product to someone they know who might get a benefit from it.

I know that I've been taken advantage of a few times, but I've gained more customers from this than it has cost me.

And you might be surprised at how many people end up coming back and buying your product in the future just because you took care of them.

Some people are also going to tell others that you took care of them quickly and in a friendly way, even if they don't buy from you again.

72 – Affiliates

Most people think of affiliates as people who own web sites and promote your products for a percentage of the sale.

If you can, you should use these types of affiliates because they do all of your marketing for you.

Look at it this way: If you invest $30 to sell a $100 product through other forms of marketing, you can afford to pay an affiliate $30 to make a $100 sale. In fact, you can often afford to pay them more because some of the people who see your product advertised by an affiliate will come direct to you and buy.

But this isn't the only type of affiliate relationship you can use. You can offer a commission to anyone who brings you customers.

One way to quickly sell more is to offer your current customers a commission for any sales they generate for you.

73 – EBay

EBay is easily one of the biggest market places on earth. They have millions of people visit their site every day looking for things to buy.

If you have any type of product you should list it on EBay.

It's easy to get started selling on EBay. All you need is a way to take pictures of your products, which you can do with a cell phone.

Sign up for an account, give a good description of your product, and include your pictures and list your products.

It's best to have a Paypal account to accept payments because this is the way most EBay shoppers pay for their purchases.

You can write a long description when you list items so make sure that you point out all of the benefits that people get from your product.

You also need to learn how to write good headlines so people can find your product on the EBay site.

EBay currently lets you list several items for free and pay a fee when they sell. This is a low cost way to offer your products to people all around the world.

The fees vary based on what type of item you sell, but I usually figure around 15% in fees on each sale. This is a combination of fees that EBay charges and that Paypal charges when you get paid.

Don't forget that you also have shipping costs when you sell products on EBay.

74 – Amazon

Amazon is probably the biggest marketplace in the world. In fact, many people won't buy a product unless it's listed on Amazon.

This doesn't mean that they always buy it from Amazon, but if a product isn't listed on the site some people are skeptical that it's a good product.

They might check it out on Amazon and buy directly from you.

The good news is that Amazon lets people list their products for sale on the site. They offer a couple different ways to offer your products so you need to do a little research to decide which way is best for you.

Just like EBay, Amazon charges a fee for selling your products based on what category they're in.

I use 15% as a rough guide to how much I pay in fees on each sale made on Amazon, but this can vary so make sure to check the fee schedule.

75 – Etsy

Etsy is another online marketplace where people list products for sale.

The site started as a place to sell crafts and similar items, but they've grown so you can offer a much wider selection of items.

Take a look at Etsy and see if there are products similar to yours for sale on the site. If there are, see if you can sell your products at a profit to their audience.

If you don't see similar products for sale on the site, ask them if you can get an account and start selling.

The fees for selling on Etsy have a wider range than when you sell on EBay or Amazon. The fees range from 10% to 25%.

Etsy does have a way that you can promote your listings for a higher fee, and this is a way to get your product in front of more people.

76 – Your Facebook Account

The odds are good that you have a Facebook account, because it seems like everyone has one.

Your Facebook page is a great place to let people know about your products or services.

You want to be careful about pushing your products too much on your Facebook page, but you definitely need to let people know what you're doing and what you have to offer.

This is also a great place to run a contest or give away free samples of your products.

You can also post ways that your customers are using your product to get benefits in their life.

Facebook also has groups that you can join. If you can offer help to people inside a group they're more likely to buy from you.

In a group make sure that you offer valuable information and help and don't come across as trying to sell something.

If you're helping people and they know that you have a product that can benefit them they're likely to come to you when they need your product.

77 – Twitter

Twitter is another form of social media that focuses on short communication and messages.

Just like when you use Facebook, focus on giving good information and solutions most of the time on your Twitter account.

Build trust with your followers and they're more likely to buy from you.

Make sure that your Twitter followers know about your products or services, but don't try to sell too much on the platform.

Give people an easy way to contact you for more information, or give them a link to your web site where they can buy your products.

78 – Your Instagram Account

Instagram is yet another form of social media that isn't used exactly the same as Facebook or Twitter.

People post pictures and videos on their Instagram account that are shown to their followers.

Instagram is a great place to show how to use your products. You can even get some of your customers to agree to let you video them using your products and post these videos on Instagram.

Focus on posting helpful information so you build trust first before you try to sell your products.

You can also place ads on most social network platforms, which you're going to learn more about in later chapters.

79 – TikTok

TikTok is a popular social media platform that focuses on short videos.

If you can show how to use your product in a short video or show the benefits of your product in a short video, TikTok has a huge user base.

If you need to use longer video you can use YouTube, which you can learn more about in the next chapter.

You don't have to be a video professional or use expensive cameras or equipment to do TikTok videos. Your cell phone is probably all that you need.

Post as much useful and valuable content as you can to build a following and build trust.

As people learn from your TikTok videos, they're going to trust you more and be more likely to buy your products.

Make sure you have a link in your profile to where people can learn more about you and your products and place orders.

80 – YouTube

YouTube is like TikTok, but you can use longer videos. You can use YouTube to really dig deep into the benefits of your product and how to use it and how it makes people's lives better.

Just like TikTok, you don't need to stress about making the perfect video or use expensive equipment.

Focus on providing valuable and useful videos so more people like them and come back for your future videos.

If you do a good job with your YouTube videos you can build a lot of trust with your followers, which leads to more sales.

Do videos that show how to solve problems and offer your product as a solution. You can also do reviews comparing your product to other products on the market.

81 – Start a Podcast

It's easy to start a podcast using services like PodBean or others. All you need to do is have a way to record your voice, and it helps to have editing software, which you can find for free.

I've used Audacity as an audio editor for many projects and I like it.

As a podcast host you're positioned as an authority, and as you've learned throughout this book, this is one of the best ways to build relationships and trust.

You can find podcasts about everything that you can think of, so you can come up with a podcast that has something to do with your product or service.

It helps if you have a good microphone, but you can get started without buying one. I've used two different microphones, one which I paid around $100 for, and another that was around $50. You don't have to spend a ton of money to get a good microphone.

82 – Internet Radio

Just like there are traditional radio stations, there are also many internet based radio stations.

While many of these internet radio stations don't have a large audience, some of them do.

Internet radio gives you two options to get the word out about your product.

The first option is to find an internet radio station that will let you do a show. A weekly show is fairly easy to do and doesn't take much time.

And this positions you as an expert just like hosting a regular radio show.

The other opportunity is placing ads on popular internet radio shows. Contact popular internet radio stations and radio show hosts that your prospects might listen to.

83 – Online Forums

Online forums aren't as popular as they used to be, but there are still active forums in most industries.

Find online forums that have something to do with your product and start posting in the forums.

You have to be careful not to look like you're just there to sell your products, so focus on being helpful and post great quality information.

The more you post and help others, the better your reputation is going to be in the forum community.

Eventually you're going to build a following who will be good prospects for your products.

Most online forums let you post a signature with every post you make where you can tell what you offer. You might even be allowed to post a link in your signature to your product or web site.

This way you're marketing and advertising your product and business every time you make a post without being pushy.

84 – Web Site

It used to take forever to launch and run a web site. The first web site I launched in 1999 took me three days to get my first page live.

Now I can put up a page in under a minute.

All you need to have your own web site is a domain name, hosting, and software to publish the pages.

Most hosting companies provide software that you can use to post your pages and run your web site.

I use Wordpress to run both my regular sites and my blogs.

Your web site can have anything that you want on it, and if you do things the right way you're going to look like an authority, which leads to more sales.

Post quality information on your web site and explain all of the benefits that your product offers. And of course, sell your products on your site.

You can also find popular web sites in your industry and see if they offer advertising on the site.

Of course, your direct competitors won't sell you ad space, but look for sites that might promote your competitors and see if you can get promoted on the same site.

85 – Blogs

A blog is a form of web site. But instead of pages, you publish posts. In the end, there isn't much difference between a web site and a blog.

You can start your own blog with a domain, hosting, and Wordpress. You can usually get all three of these things at the same place.

You don't need expensive hosting or an expensive domain name. You can buy domain names for around $10 a year and hosting for $5 a month or less to get started.

If you decide to start a blog instead of a more traditional web site it's helpful to post on a regular basis.

If you don't want to post on a regular basis you should do a regular web site. You should still add new information often, but you don't have to follow a schedule.

Just like with regular web sites, you can approach popular blogs to see if you can place an ad to drive sales.

86 – Guest Articles Online

Some owners of web sites and blogs are looking for good content to put on their sites. If you can write a quality article you can find places that will post your article for free.

When you do a guest article or post you need to focus on offering the best information that you can.

Make sure that you can post a link to your product or site and include a short paragraph at the end of the article telling who you are and what you have to offer.

This is a win-win situation because the site owner gets a piece of good content for free and you get free publicity for your product.

It might take some work to find sites that accept guest articles and posts, but as you work at it you can build a list of places to get free marketing in the future.

All you have to do is write another article. You can also buy articles to use this way if you don't like to write, or aren't a good writer.

87 – Guest on Podcasts

One of the best ways to get a fast boost in sales is to appear as a guest on a popular podcast.

Many podcasts are done in an interview format where the host interviews people on every podcast.

Competition to get on the most popular podcasts is fierce, so start trying to land guest spots on podcasts that have a following but haven't quite made it big yet.

The podcast host isn't going to want to talk too much about your product, but they are going to be interested in information that helps their audience.

Figure out things you can talk about that offer value to the podcast host and their audience. The main thing is to offer good information and present it in an interesting way.

Finding opportunities to be a guest on podcasts just takes time and effort. If you put in the work you can find guest opportunities.

88 – Guest on Radio

Another way to position yourself as an expert is to appear as a guest on radio shows in your local market, or even on a national level.

Plenty of radio programs have guests, and radio stations are always looking for quality content to offer their audience.

Listen to your local radio stations to identify the programs that have guests. Figure out a way to offer information as a guest that has something to do with your product or service.

You're not going to be able to be in selling mode too much when you guest on a radio show, but you can find ways to work your product or service into the conversation.

Start contacting radio stations to see what they're looking for, and then figure out how to give them what they want.

You might also explore the opportunity to do your own local radio show once a week if the radio station has open programming spots.

89 – Guest on TV

Just about everything that you just learned in the guest on radio chapter applies to being a guest on TV.

If you're willing to build your knowledge about something that offers valuable content to a television audience you can land guest TV spots. It just takes work and effort to find places that are looking for guests.

You can also learn how to be recognized as an authority about a subject and let TV news shows know that you're available as a guest expert.

This takes a little more work, but you can get a lot of free publicity this way. And because the TV news show is going to tell the audience that you're an expert, the audience is going to look at you like an expert.

Many local television stations also have open programming spots where you might be able to do your own show.

90 – Start an Ezine

An ezine is simply a newsletter that you send by email. This is an inexpensive way to send a newsletter because you can send emails for free.

The easiest way to do this is by using an autoresponder software program where people can sign up and you can send the same email to all of them at once.

You want to offer a lot of good information in your ezine that cements your status as an expert.

This information can be anything to do with your product or industry, and can include things that are only loosely related to your industry as long as the information is of value.

Your ezine doesn't have to be long. If you can put together at least four pages of good information on a regular basis you can launch your ezine.

When you launch make sure to let everyone you know what you're doing and ask them to forward your ezine to anyone they think can benefit from it.

Of course, your ezine is the perfect place to include information about how your product or service improves people's lives.

Remember to focus on the benefits to your customers for each of your products.

91 – Ezine Ads

You can also find popular ezines that have already built a following and buy an ad in them.

You can use an ezine ad to directly advertise your products or services or you can advertise your new ezine or web site.

Ezines aren't as popular as they once were, but there are still some with large followings.

A newer form of this is people that have a list of followers and they just send short emails to them.

You can also find people that have a list they use this way and see if they will sell you an ad to their list.

92 – Build an App

Cell phones and computers use apps for all kinds of things, and some apps are so popular that millions of people use them.

It's a little more challenging to build an app than a simple web site or blog, but plenty of people know how to build apps.

It might take some brainstorming to figure out an idea for a useful app that somehow ties into your product or service, but if you can, you have the opportunity to build a big audience fast.

You can find stores for apps where you can offer your new app. Do a search for app stores to see all of the places where you might be able to place your app.

When you build an app, try to build a version for Android phones and for iPhones. This way you can get maximum coverage.

93 – Answer Questions Online

You can find several sites on the internet where people post questions and other people can post answers.

These are good places to look to add valuable answers that people read now and in the future.

You have to learn how to work your product or service in without appearing to be a pushy sales person, but as long as you give good answers you can learn how to do this and boost your sales.

94 – Post in Online Groups

I mentioned in an earlier section about Facebook the power of joining and posting in groups. Facebook isn't the only place to find groups online.

All you have to do is do a search for groups that have something to do with your product or service.

For example, if you sell auto parts you can search for car groups or auto enthusiast groups. If you sell financial products you could search for finance groups.

Look for groups that are active. A group doesn't have to have 1,000's of members to be active, but the bigger the group the more marketing bang for your buck you'll get.

Spend some time becoming a trusted member of the group at first. Provide as much help and good information as you can and build your reputation.

95 – Online Directories

Online directories used to be used by many people to find sites that people were looking for as much as people used search engines.

Now most people use search engines, but there are still a few online directories that can send you potential customers.

You need to build a web site and put quite a bit of valuable information on it to get accepted in some of the good online directories.

But once you get your site in, your listing can send you new customers. And as a side benefit, many online directory links help you improve your rankings in search engines.

96 – Ads on Google

Google is currently the biggest search engine in the world. They weren't always the biggest, but it looks like they're going to remain the biggest for a long time.

Google will sell you ads that are placed along with search results, which can help you target exactly the prospects that you're looking for.

You're going to need to test different ads and different target groups to find profitable combinations, but Google has more traffic than you can handle.

Start with a small ad budget and test as much as you can. When an ad and target market proves profitable you can increase your budget to reach more people.

97 – Ads on Yahoo

Yahoo is another popular search engine, but they're not as big as Google. They also offer advertising that shows up alongside their search results, as well as other advertising opportunities.

Plenty of people still use Yahoo, though their traffic is lower than Google's. It's a good network to test ads on with a small budget.

Once you make an ad run profitably on Yahoo, the odds are good that you can make the same ad run profitably on Google.

Some of the traffic on Yahoo is the same as you find on Google, but for the most part Yahoo is a different market than Google.

This means that you can run a successful ad on both platforms to increase your sales more.

98 – Ads on MSN

The third main search engine is MSN, and everything that you just learned about Yahoo is basically true for MSN.

MSN offers ads that appear in search results as well as other advertising opportunities.

I like to test ads on MSN, Yahoo, and Google with small budgets to see which network is the most profitable.

You need to know that advertising on the main search engines can provide a lot of value, but it can be hard to figure out how to make ads profitable at first.

You need to make sure that you don't waste too much money when you're testing, and you have to learn from every ad and group or target that doesn't return a profit.

But if you stick with it and keep learning, you can learn how to sell a large number of products on these search engines.

99 – Facebook Ads

Facebook has as much traffic as any web site, and you can tap into this traffic by running ads on the network.

Facebook makes it easy to buy ads, but you need to do some work to make sure you're targeting the ads to the best people for your product or service.

The good news is that if you can build a customer profile in your mind, Facebook can deliver your ad to only people that match what you're looking for.

If your target customer is between 40 and 49 years old, female, and is a business owner, you can only show your ads to women that meet these requirements.

You might need to test a lot of different ads and targets, but Facebook ads can help you sell a lot of products or services once you figure out the most profitable ways to use the platform.

100 – Instagram Ads

Instagram is owned by Facebook and you can place ads on Instagram using the Facebook ad area.

While it seems like everyone in the world is on Facebook, the truth is that not everyone is. And some people use Instagram for a different reason than they use Facebook.

If you develop ads that work well on Facebook you should test the same ads on Instagram.

Running successful ads for your products, especially online, requires testing and tweaking based on your results.

An ad that works in one place might work well in another, or you might have to change a few things to make it successful.

The only way to know is run ads, test ads, and learn as you get more information.

For Entrepreneurs Only

Congratulations! Now you know how to sell and where to sell. All you have to do is put what you just learned into action.

If all you're interested in is learning about the 100 ways to sell, you can stop reading now.

But if you're an entrepreneur, or want to start your own business, I have something else to share with you.

I work in a consulting role with a few entrepreneurs in addition to running my own business ventures.

If you're looking for someone to lead you to figuring everything out yourself, I'm not your guy. That is what coaches do.

When I see something that can help someone I'm working with make more money and make their business more successful, I tell them what to do.

In other words, if you're looking for experienced help that's been there and done that and is going to tell you the truth, you should reach out to me to see if I have any openings.

You need to know that it's not cheap to work with me. I run my businesses and any time I spend consulting takes me away from them. My current rate is $1,000 an hour for consulting work.

You can consider this expensive if you choose to, but it's a bargain if I help you make multiples of that, like I do with my clients.

If you're ready to take your business to the next level, send me an email letting me know that you're interested, including as much information as you can about your business and where you want to go with your business, and I'll let you know if I have any openings and what the next step is.

You can reach me at wesyoungbusiness@gmail.com

www.ingramcontent.com/pod-product-compliance
Lightning Source LLC
Chambersburg PA
CBHW060548200326
41521CB00007B/526